DOGS ON THE JOB

POLICE DOGS

by Tammy Gagne

Consultant:
Gary Garrison
North American Police Work Dog Association

CAPSTONE PRESS
a capstone imprint

Edge Books are published by Capstone Press,
1710 Roe Crest Drive, North Mankato, Minnesota 56003
www.capstonepub.com

Library of Congress Cataloging-in-Publication Data
Gagne, Tammy.
Police dogs / by Tammy Gagne.
pages cm.—(Edge books. Dogs on the job)
Includes index.
ISBN 978-1-4765-0129-1 (library binding)
ISBN 978-1-4765-3385-8 (ebook PDF)
1. Police dogs—Juvenile literature. 2. Police dogs—United States—Juvenile literature.
I. Title.
HV8025.G24 2014
363.28—dc23   2012051696

Editorial Credits
Brenda Haugen, editor; Kyle Grenz, designer; Marcie Spence, media researcher;
Laura Manthe, production specialist

Photo Credits
Adam Hester Visuals, 20; AP Images: Chris Court/PA Wire URN: 5780340 Press
Association, 24, *The State Journal-Register*, Jason Johnson, 8; Capstone Studio: Karon
Dubke, 10, 11; Dreamstime: Supersport, 28; Fotolia: Canadeez, 16, Michael Ireland,
29; Getty Images: Universal History Archive, 6; Minnesota House of Representatives:
Tom Olmscheid, 21; Newscom: David Cruz, 4, Erin Tracy/ZUMA Press, 19, Matt
Stewart/ZUMA Press, cover, Rob Swanson/ZUMA Press, 18, Saul Loeb/AFP/Getty
Images, 9; Peter Casolino/New Haven Register, 14; Shutterstock: Billy Gadbury, 23,
Chuck Rausin, 22, Kachalkina Veronika, 12, 26-27, KellyNelson, 13, Marcel Jancovic,
25, Monika Wisniewska, 7, Rolf Klebsattel, 5

Printed in the United States of America in Stevens Point, Wisconsin.
032013   007227WZF13

Table of Contents

CHAPTER 1

Loyal Partners

Washington, D.C., Police Officer William Gregory and his **canine** partner, Dylan, were working their regular midnight shift. Suddenly things took a dangerous turn. A man flagged them down asking for help. He said that another man had just tried to rob him at gunpoint.

Dogs are valued members of many police forces.

canine—to do with dogs
suspect—someone thought to be responsible for a crime

Gregory quickly found the **suspect** and told him to stop. The man chose to run instead. Gregory released Dylan, who raced after the man. The suspect fired his gun at the dog. Dylan fell to the ground, rolled over, and got back up. Dylan kept running after the man who had just shot him.

FACT

Police dogs follow orders, even if it means risking their lives to do so.

The suspect shot Dylan two more times before Gregory caught up with him and returned fire. The dog lay on the ground in a pool of blood as the suspect was arrested. But Dylan survived. He was treated at a nearby veterinary hospital and released a few days later.

The first police dog program was created in Ghent, Belgium, in 1899. The dogs were German shepherds. These dogs had long been **bred** for herding cattle and sheep. This work made German shepherds excellent protectors.

Ghent police used dogs to guard important places and control crowds. As guard dogs, they could attack suspects who tried to break into buildings. If a crowd of people became unruly, simply the dogs' presence helped prevent a **riot** from happening. Most people will back down from a K-9 team more quickly than just a human officer alone.

breed—to mate and produce young; a person who breeds and raises animals to sell is called a breeder

riot—a large gathering of people who use violence to show their anger

Soon police departments in other countries developed K-9 programs. The first police dogs were used in the United States in the early 1900s. Police dogs worked in New York City in 1907 and in New Haven, Connecticut, in 1910. Over time the dogs' duties expanded. Dogs tracked criminals. They also sniffed out bombs and illegal drugs.

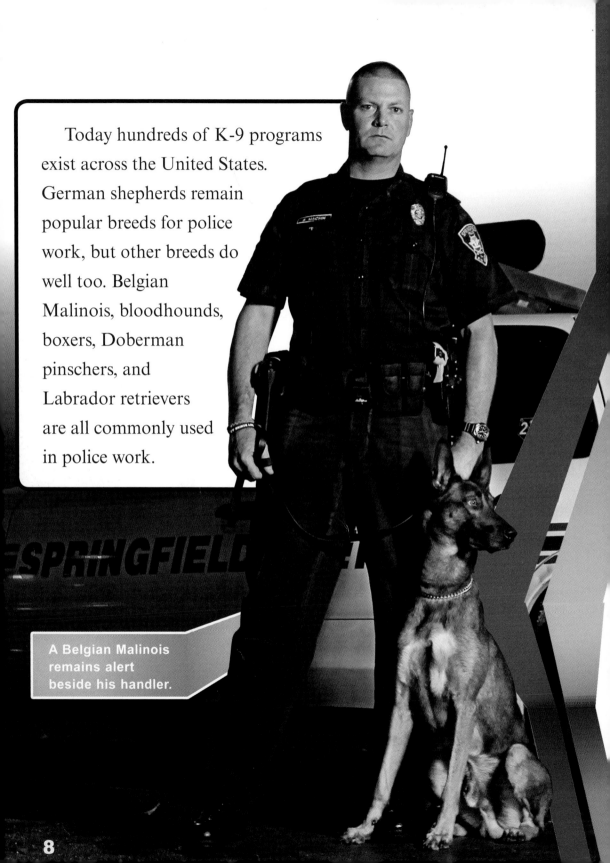

Today hundreds of K-9 programs exist across the United States. German shepherds remain popular breeds for police work, but other breeds do well too. Belgian Malinois, bloodhounds, boxers, Doberman pinschers, and Labrador retrievers are all commonly used in police work.

A Belgian Malinois remains alert beside his handler.

A police officer and his or her K-9 partner often **patrol** a certain area. They may patrol in a vehicle or on foot. Both partners are always on the lookout for anything unusual. In addition to their strong sense of smell, dogs have especially good hearing. Using these senses, dogs can often find criminals before their human partners can. Following a crime, police dogs may help gather **evidence** or find stolen property. They may also chase down suspects who try to run away. Police dogs can run faster than people. Even the most athletic criminals are no match for a dog.

Gender Is No Barrier

Most police dogs are male, but female dogs also make great K-9 partners. Deputy Jeff VanHoos and Jaro are a K-9 team from Sangamon County, Illinois. In 2009 Jaro won first place at a U.S. Police Canine Association field trials event. She was the first female dog to earn the honor.

patrol—to protect and watch an area

evidence—information, items, and facts that help prove something is true or false

CHAPTER 2

The Best Dog for the Job

To be part of a K-9 police team, a dog must be smart, friendly, and curious. It is also important for a police dog to be **obedient**. The human officer must be able to count on his or her canine partner to follow commands.

obedient—able to follow rules and commands

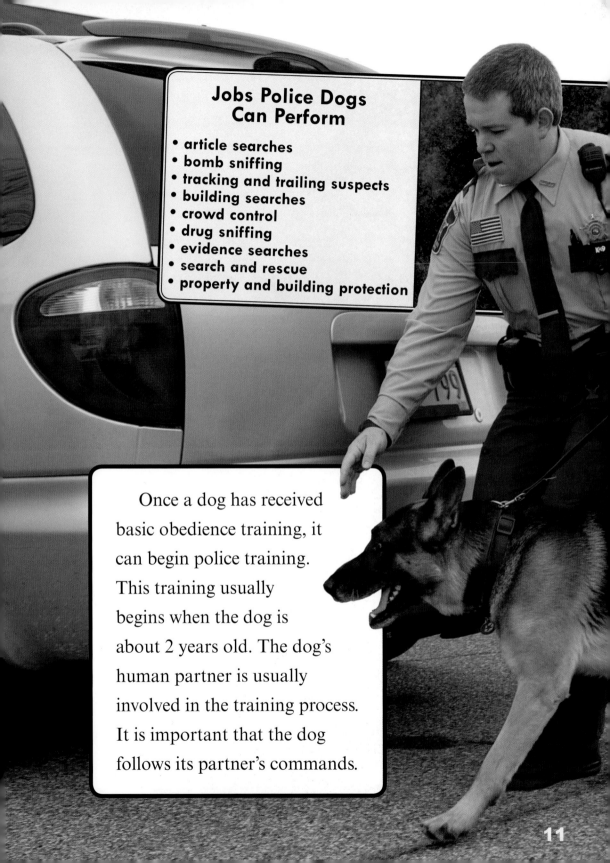

Jobs Police Dogs Can Perform

- article searches
- bomb sniffing
- tracking and trailing suspects
- building searches
- crowd control
- drug sniffing
- evidence searches
- search and rescue
- property and building protection

Once a dog has received basic obedience training, it can begin police training. This training usually begins when the dog is about 2 years old. The dog's human partner is usually involved in the training process. It is important that the dog follows its partner's commands.

During training, dogs go with their handlers to **firing ranges**. Most police officers rarely fire their weapons. But when police use their guns, their K-9 partners must remain calm. A dog that is scared by gunfire cannot serve as a police dog.

During training a handler teaches a dog to climb over high structures and crawl through small spaces. The dog also learns to jump through open windows. All K-9 officers must learn to track suspects or missing persons. Many police dogs are also taught how to sniff for bombs, drugs, or guns.

firing range—a place where people can practice shooting weapons

About half the dogs that go through training become police dogs. During training it quickly becomes clear when a dog is not right for police work. Dogs that are too shy, too excited, or easily distracted are dropped from the police dog program. Though they may not be right for police work, dogs that fail training usually make wonderful pets.

FACT

A police dog can search a vehicle in about three minutes.

an officer and canine training on a course

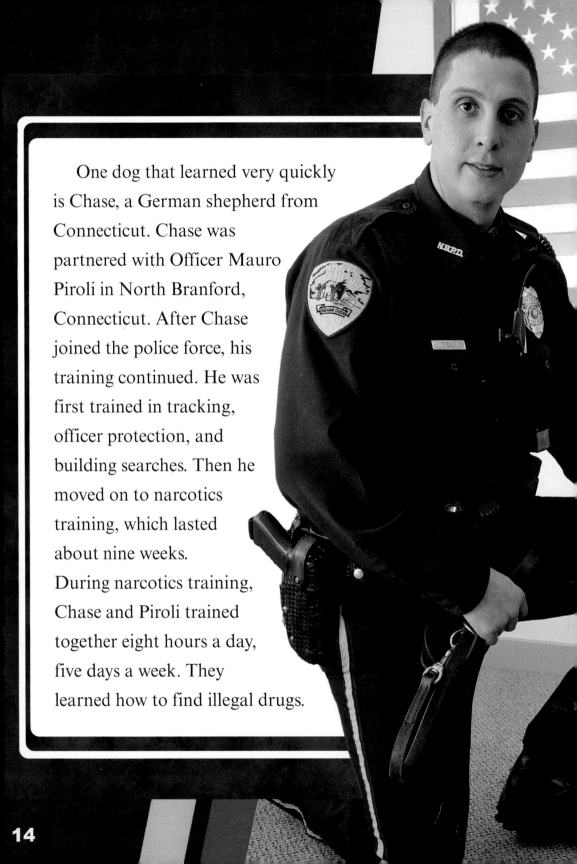

One dog that learned very quickly is Chase, a German shepherd from Connecticut. Chase was partnered with Officer Mauro Piroli in North Branford, Connecticut. After Chase joined the police force, his training continued. He was first trained in tracking, officer protection, and building searches. Then he moved on to narcotics training, which lasted about nine weeks. During narcotics training, Chase and Piroli trained together eight hours a day, five days a week. They learned how to find illegal drugs.

Training a police dog isn't just time consuming. It is costly. Police departments invest in special equipment for K-9 programs. For example, Piroli's vehicle is specially designed. The vehicle has a remote system. The system lets Piroli open a door from up to 1,000 feet (305 meters) away. If he is not near the vehicle but needs Chase's help, Piroli just presses a button to open the door. Chase can jump out of the vehicle and hurry to help his partner.

Officer Mauro Piroli and Chase

CHAPTER 3

On Patrol

An Italian police dog showed just how useful K-9 officers can be in March 1958. Salvatore Suriano was robbing a jewelry store in Rome when he was interrupted. He had planned to break into the store through the basement of the movie theater next door.

What he had not counted on was that a guard at the theater would hear him. The burglar sneaked into the theater's basement. The theater guard went to the basement when he heard a noise. The burglar jumped on the guard from behind. The two men fought. Fearing someone might hear them, Suriano ran away.

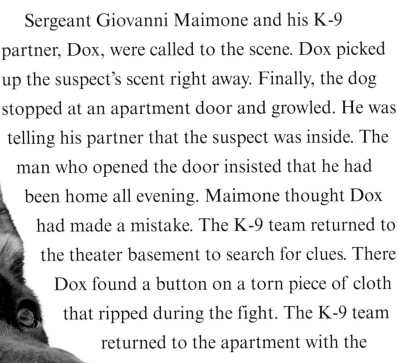

Sergeant Giovanni Maimone and his K-9 partner, Dox, were called to the scene. Dox picked up the suspect's scent right away. Finally, the dog stopped at an apartment door and growled. He was telling his partner that the suspect was inside. The man who opened the door insisted that he had been home all evening. Maimone thought Dox had made a mistake. The K-9 team returned to the theater basement to search for clues. There Dox found a button on a torn piece of cloth that ripped during the fight. The K-9 team returned to the apartment with the evidence. Dox ran to a closet and started barking. Inside the closet, Maimone found a coat that was missing the fabric and button in his hand. Suriano confessed, and Maimone arrested him for the attempted burglary.

Like this dog, Dox was a German shepherd.

Many K-9 officers work just as hard as human officers. Both put in about 16 hours a month of ongoing training. This training keeps their skills sharp. But it is important that the dogs get free time too.

Just like their human partners, police dogs put their lives at risk while doing their jobs. A suspect may have a gun, a knife, or another weapon and use it to attack a dog while fleeing.

Protecting Police Dogs

Most police departments do not have enough money to buy bulletproof vests for their dogs. Vested Interest in K-9s, Inc. is a group working to solve this issue. The group provides K-9 units with the protective gear they need.

Deputy Stephen Miller's K-9 partner, Kilo, was given one of these vests. Miller and Kilo were searching for a suspect who had shot at another officer on August 2, 2010. When Kilo found the suspect, the man shot the dog multiple times. Kilo survived, likely because of his vest. Point Blank Vest Company, which had made the vest, provided Kilo with a new one. Police departments hope that as more dogs are provided with bulletproof vests, dog injury and death rates will decrease.

Police also risk getting in car accidents while chasing suspects. On December 26, 2008, Officer Brent Ambuel and his K-9 partner, Hunter, were going to a call in Colorado Springs, Colorado. Ambuel had his lights and siren on. But another driver failed to stop for the police car. The person's car crashed into the police vehicle, which flipped over. Ambuel was taken to a hospital. Hunter was sent to a vet clinic. Ambuel was released the same day, but it took Hunter about two weeks to recover.

Officer John Jorgensen's K-9 partner, Major, wasn't so lucky when he was injured on the job. An alarm had gone off at a truck parts company, and the K-9 team was called to the scene in Roseville, Minnesota. Major went into the woods to search for the suspect. Suddenly Jorgensen heard the dog cry out. He found Major a few minutes later. Major had been stabbed four times.

FACT

A Miami, Florida, police dog named Brit was given a full police funeral in 1997.

Jorgensen rushed Major to a nearby vet, but the damage was severe. Major's spinal cord and one of his lungs was damaged. Major survived the attack, but he was unable to move his back legs. Major still gets around with the help of a canine wheelchair. He now serves his community by visiting schools with Jorgensen.

Jorgensen and Major's story led Minnesota lawmakers to pass a new law. Harming a police dog in Minnesota is now punishable by up to two years in prison.

CHAPTER 4

Life in Retirement

Most K-9 teams become very close. Officers work and train with their dogs. Most K-9 teams also live together. Spending so much time together creates a strong bond.

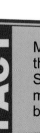

FACT

Most police dogs stay with their handlers after they **retire**. Sometimes even younger dogs must retire if they get sick or become injured.

But being a police dog is hard work. As a dog gets older, it's harder for the animal to do its job. When a dog enters its senior years, its human partner must think about the dog's retirement. Signs that a dog should retire include slowing **reflexes** and an inability to jump as high as it once did.

retire—to give up work, usually because of age
reflex—an action that happens without control or effort

A large statue of a police dog stands in Byram Park in Greenwich, Connecticut. The sculpture was modeled after Yogi, the town's first police dog.

Most police dogs retire by age 8 or 9. But Sergeant Kevin Canady's K-9 partner, Ringo, was still working in Kinston, North Carolina, at 13. A Belgian Malinois, Ringo tracked down a robbery suspect his first day on the job. During the rest of his career, Ringo helped Canady catch many dangerous criminals.

A two-wheeled harness helps this injured police dog get around during retirement.

Once Ringo entered his teens, he started slowing down. He could no longer work 12-hour days. Instead, he worked for six hours at a time. He also performed at the Kinston Department of Public Safety Range. There Ringo showed the public what police dogs can do. Even though Ringo was a senior at the time, he was still tough. The person who played the role of the criminal at the shows had to wear special gear to avoid getting hurt.

A handler wears protective gear so he is not hurt while giving a demonstration with his dog.

Keeping retired police dogs busy is important. Suddenly having nothing to do all day can cause behavior problems for retired dogs. These animals often enjoy canine sports such as agility and flyball. Officer Kevin Halsey and his K-9 partner Riley worked together for seven years in Warwick, New York. When Riley suffered a back injury, he had to retire earlier than planned. Halsey knew that not going to work would be hard for Riley. He also worried about how Riley was going to react to his new police dog, Nicky.

A dog climbs steps at an agility training field.

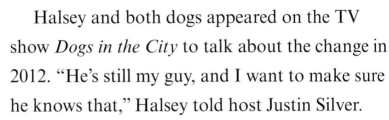

Halsey and both dogs appeared on the TV show *Dogs in the City* to talk about the change in 2012. "He's still my guy, and I want to make sure he knows that," Halsey told host Justin Silver. " … but I also have to … **socialize** him with my family as well." Halsey let his son, Nathan, help. Nathan made sure Riley got exercise and attention when Halsey and Nicky were on patrol.

socialize—to train to get along with people and other dogs

FACT

More than 50,000 police dogs work in the United States. It costs about $16,000 to train each K-9 officer and its handler.

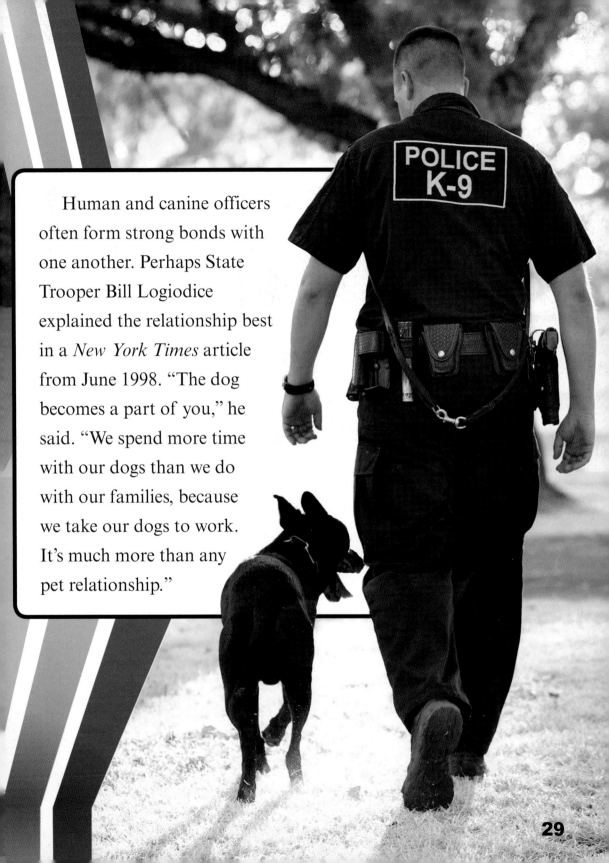

Human and canine officers often form strong bonds with one another. Perhaps State Trooper Bill Logiodice explained the relationship best in a *New York Times* article from June 1998. "The dog becomes a part of you," he said. "We spend more time with our dogs than we do with our families, because we take our dogs to work. It's much more than any pet relationship."

Glossary

breed (BREED)—to mate and produce young; a person who breeds and raises animals to sell is called a breeder

canine (KAY-nyn)—to do with dogs

evidence (E-vuh-duhnts)—information, items, and facts that help prove something is true or false

firing range (FYE-ring RAYNJ)—a place where people can practice shooting weapons

obedient (oh-BEE-dee-uhnt)—able to follow rules and commands

patrol (puh-TROHL)—to protect and watch an area

reflex (REE-fleks)—an action that happens without control or effort

retire (ri-TIRE)—to give up work, usually because of age

riot (RYE-uht)—a large gathering of people who use violence to show their anger

socialize (SOH-shuh-lize)—to train to get along with people and other dogs

suspect (SUHSS-pekt)—someone thought to be responsible for a crime

Read More

Bozzo, Linda. *Police Dog Heroes*. Berkeley Heights, N.J.: Enslow Publishers, 2011.

Gagne, Tammy. *German Shepherds*. Mankato, Minn.: Capstone Press, 2009.

Hoffman, Mary Ann. *Police Dogs*. New York: Gareth Stevens Pub., 2011.

Internet Sites

FactHound offers a safe, fun way to find Internet sites related to this book. All of the sites on FactHound have been researched by our staff.

Here's all you do:

Visit *www.facthound.com*

Type in this code: 9781476501291

Super-cool stuff!

Check out projects, games and lots more at
www.capstonekids.com

Index